KNOCK KNOCK

JOKES

FOR

KIDS

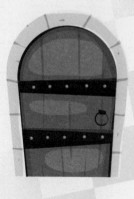

ARCTURUS

Knock, knock ...
Who's there?
Jurgen ...
Jurgen who?
**Jurgen to love this
Knock, knock book!**

ARCTURUS

This edition published in 2019 by Arcturus Publishing Limited
26/27 Bickels Yard, 151–153 Bermondsey Street,
London SE1 3HA

Author: Joe King
Jacket illustrator: Lyudmyla Kharlamova at Shutterstock
Interiors illustrator: Genie Espinosa
Editor: Kait Eaton at Duck Egg Blue
Designer: Duck Egg Blue

ISBN: 978-1-78950-405-7
CH007212NT
Supplier 29, Date 0719, Print run 8468

Printed in China

CONTENTS

FUNNY JOKES!

Knock, knock ...
Who's there?
Howie ...
Howie who?
**I'm fine thanks.
How are you?**

Knock, knock ...
Who's there?
Arnold ...
Arnold who?
Arnold friend you haven't seen for years!

Knock, knock ...
Who's there?
Lisa ...
Lisa who?
Lisa you can do is let me in!

Knock, knock ...
Who's there?
Dot ...
Dot who?
Dots for me to know, and you to find out!

Knock, knock ...
Who's there?
Avon ...
Avon who?
Avon to drink your blood!

5

Knock, knock ...
Who's there?
Datsun ...
Datsun who?
**Datsun old
joke!**

Knock, knock ...
Who's there?
May ...
May who?
**May the force be
with you!**

Knock, knock ...
Who's there?
Dime ...
Dime who?
**Dime to tell another
knock, knock joke!**

Knock, knock ...
Who's there?
House ...
House who?
House you doing!

Knock, knock ...
Who's there?
Ben ...
Ben who?
Ben skiing lately?

Knock, knock ...
Who's there?
Atilla ...
Atilla who?
**Atilla you open this door I'm a
gonna stand here!**

Knock, knock ...
Who's there?
Toby ...
Toby who?
Toby or not to be!

Knock, knock ...
Who's there?
Curry ...
Curry who?
**Curry me home, please.
My legs are tired!**

Knock, knock ...
Who's there?
Betty ...
Betty who?
**Betty ya don't
know who this is!**

Knock, knock ...
Who's there?
Dawn ...
Dawn who?
Dawn leave me out here in the cold!

Knock, knock!
Who's there?
Al ...
Al who?
**Al huff and I'll puff and blow your
house down!**

Knock, knock ...
Who's there?
Maxwell ...
Maxwell who?
**Maxwell call later—
he asked me to let
you know!**

9

Knock, knock ...
Who's there?
Howard ...
Howard who?
Howard can it be to guess a knock, knock joke?

Knock, knock ...
Who's there?
Larva ...
Larva who?
Larva cup of coffee, thank you!

Knock, knock ...
Who's there?
Cologne ...
Cologne who?
Cologne me names won't help!

Knock, knock ...
Who's there?
Holly ...
Holly who?
Hollylujah!

Knock, knock ...
Who's there?
Hutch ...
Hutch who?
Bless you!

Knock, knock ...
Who's there?
Chile ...
Chile who?
**Chile out tonight,
isn't it?**

Knock, knock ...
Who's there?
Butter ...
Butter who?
**Butter not leave me here
much longer!**

Knock, knock ...
Who's there?
Closure ...
Closure who?
Closure mouth when you're eating!

Knock knock ...
Who's there?
Dishes ...
Dishes who?
Dishes me.
Who's that?

Knock, knock ...
Who's there?
Minerva ...
Minerva who?
Minerva-s wreck
from all these
questions!

Knock, knock ...
Who's there?
Luke ...
Luke who?
Luke through
the keyhole and
you'll see!

Knock, knock ...
Who's there?
Chester ...
Chester who?
Chester the nick of time!

Knock, knock ...
Who's there?
Heaven ...
Heaven who?
Heaven seen you in ages!

Knock, knock ...
Who's there?
Amahl ...
Amahl who?
Amahl shook up!

Knock, knock ...
Who's there?
Saturn ...
Saturn who?
Saturn my spaceship, waiting to take off!

Knock, knock ...
Who's there?
Disguise ...
Disguise who?
Disguise the limit!

Knock, knock ...
Who's there?
Iowa ...
Iowa who?
Iowa you some money!

15

Knock, knock ...
Who's there?
Jerrold ...
Jerrold who?
Jerrold friend, that's who!

Knock, knock ...
Who's there?
Ivor ...
Ivor who?
Ivor good mind not to tell you now!

Knock, knock ...
Who's there?
Hanover ...
Hanover who?
Hanover your money!

Knock, knock ...
Who's there?
Falafel ...
Falafel who?
**Falafel off my bike
and hurt my knee!**

Knock, knock ...
Who's there?
Denise ...
Denise who?
Denise are above de ankles!

Knock, knock ...
Who's there?
Joan ...
Joan who?
Joan call us—we'll call you!

Knock, knock ...
Who's there?
June ...
June who?
June know what time dinner is?

Knock, knock!

Knock, knock ...
Who's there?
Alf ...
Alf who?
Alf feed your cat
while you're away!

Knock, knock ...
Who's there?
Ooze ...
Ooze who?
Ooze in charge
round here?

Knock, knock ...
Who's there?
Ivory ...
Ivory who?
Ivory strong, just like Tarzan!

Knock, knock ...
Who's there?
Juanita ...
Juanita who?
Juanita nother burger?

Knock, knock ...
Who's there?
Fonda ...
Fonda who?
Fonda you!

Knock, knock ...
Who's there?
Wood ...
Wood who?
Wood you like to let me in now?

Knock, knock ...
Who's there?
Harmon ...
Harmon who?
Harmon on your side!

Knock, knock ...
Who's there?
Ali ...
Ali who?
Alligator. Or maybe crocodile. I can't really tell the difference!

Knock, knock ...
Who's there?
Julie ...
Julie who?
Julie-ve your door unlocked?

Knock, knock ...
Who's there?
Carla ...
Carla who?
Carla restaurant, I'm hungry!

Knock, knock ...
Who's there?
Quacker ...
Quacker who?
Quacker another bad
joke and I'm leaving!

Knock, knock ...
Who's there?
Justice ...
Justice who?
Justice as I thought, there's no-one home!

Knock, knock ...
Who's there?
Cyril ...
Cyril who?
Cyril nice to meet you!

Knock, knock ...
Who's there?
Hank ...
Hank who?
No, hank you!

Knock, knock ...
Who's there?
Harold ...
Harold who?
Harold are you?

Knock, knock ...
Who's there?
Plato ...
Plato who?
Plato fish and chips, please!

EVEN FUNNIER JOKES!

Knock, knock ...
Who's there?
Eileen ...
Eileen who?
**Eileen down to tie my shoe
and fell over!**

Knock, knock ...
Who's there?
Pizza ...
Pizza who?
Pizza the pie!

Knock, knock ...
Who's there?
Ken ...
Ken who?
Ken you come out
to play?

Knock, knock ...
Who's there?
Ken ...
Ken who?
Ken I come in, or do I have to climb
through a window?

Knock, knock ...
Who's there?
Ken ...
Ken who?
Ken you stop locking me out? This
is the third time I've had to knock!

Knock, knock ...
Who's there?
Collier ...
Collier who?
Collier big brother then, see if I care!

Knock, knock ...
Who's there?
Jaws ...
Jaws who?
Jaws truly!

Knock, knock ...
Who's there?
Irma ...
Irma who?
Irma big girl now!

Knock, knock ...
Who's there?
Doris ...
Doris who?
Doris slammed on my finger. Ouch!

Knock, knock ...
Who's there?
Ivan ...
Ivan who?
Ivan to come in, please open the door!

Knock, knock ...
Who's there?
Oliver ...
Oliver who?
Oliver–cross the road from you!

Knock, knock ...
Who's there?
Little old lady ...
Little old lady who?
I didn't know you could yodel!

Knock, knock ...
Who's there?
Evan ...
Evan who?
**Evan you should know
who it is!**

Knock, knock ...
Who's there?
Gladys ...
Gladys who?
**Gladys the weekend,
aren't you!**

Knock, knock ...
Who's there?
Jools ...
Jools who?
Jools like these should be worth a lot of money!

Knock, knock ...
Who's there?
Alec ...
Alec who?
Alec my lollipop, you lick yours!

Knock, knock ...
Who's there?
Isaac ...
Isaac who?
Isaac'ly who do think this is?

Knock, knock ...
Who's there?
Zizi ...
Zizi who?
Zizi when you
know how!

Knock, knock ...
Who's there?
Grant ...
Grant who?
Grant you a wish—
what is it?

Knock, knock ...
Who's there?
Anita ...
Anita who?
Anita nother
hot dog—I'm starving!

30

Knock, knock ...
Who's there?
Goat ...
Goat who?
Goat to the door and
find out!

Knock,
knock!

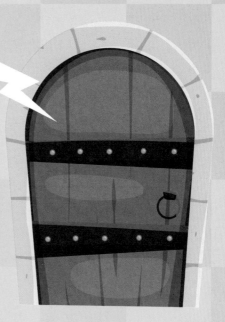

Knock, knock ...
Who's there?
Len ...
Len who?
Len us some
money, will you?

Knock, knock ...
Who's there?
Harry ...
Harry who?
Harry up and answer this door!

Knock, knock ...
Who's there?
Goodunov ...
Goodunov who?
Goodunov to eat!

Knock, knock ...
Who's there?
Livia ...
Livia who?
Livia me alone!

Knock, knock ...
Who's there?
Aladdin ...
Aladdin who?
Aladdin the street wants a word with you!

Knock, knock ...
Who's there?
Annie ...
Annie who?
Annie chance of getting something to eat?

Knock, knock ...
Who's there?
Havana ...
Havana who?
**Havana a great time.
Wish you were here!**

Knock, knock ...
Who's there?
Conga ...
Conga who?
Conga go on meeting like this!

33

Knock, knock ...
Who's there?
Arthur ...
Arthur who?
Arthur any cookies left?

Knock, knock ...
Who's there?
Heart ...
Heart who?
**Heart to hear you—
speak up!**

Knock, knock ...
Who's there?
Europe ...
Europe who?
**Europe-ning the door
too slow, come on!**

Knock, knock ...
Who's there?
Holland ...
Holland who?
Holland you going to make me
wait out here?

Knock, knock ...
Who's there?
Norway ...
Norway who?
Norway will I leave until
you open this door!

Knock, knock ...
Who's there?
Germany ...
Germany who?
Germany people knock
on your door?

35

Knock, knock ...
Who's there?
Major ...
Major who?
Major answer didn't I!

Knock, knock ...
Who's there?
Maura ...
Maura who?
The Maura the merrier!

Knock, knock ...
Who's there?
Arthur ...
Arthur who?
Arthur minute and I'll show you my identification!

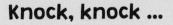

Knock, knock ...
Who's there?
Carrie ...
Carrie who?
**Carrie one of these boxes
for me, will you?**

Knock, knock ...
Who's there?
Iris ...
Iris who?
Iris you were here!

Knock, knock ...
Who's there?
Ice cream soda ...
Ice cream soda who?
**Ice cream soda people
can hear me!**

Knock, knock ...
Who's there?
Aware ...
Aware who?
Aware, aware has my little dog gone?

Knock, knock!

Knock, knock ...
Who's there?
Tank ...
Tank who?
You're welcome!

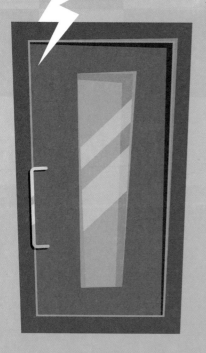

Knock, knock ...
Who's there?
Argue ...
Argue who?
Argue going to let me in or not?

Knock, knock ...
Who's there?
Giraffe ...
Giraffe who?
Giraffe to sit right in front of me?

Knock, knock ...
Who's there?
Iona ...
Iona who?
Iona pony. Do you have any pets?

Knock, knock ...
Who's there?
Mayor ...
Mayor who?
Mayor come in?

Knock, knock ...
Who's there?
Cathy ...
Cathy who?
**Cathy the doorbell, it's too
dark out here!**

Knock, knock ...
Who's there?
Yul ...
Yul who?
**Yul see when you
open the door!**

40

Knock, knock ...
Who's there?
Henrietta ...
Henrietta who?
**Henrietta big dinner and now
he feels sick!**

Knock, knock ...
Who's there?
Philip ...
Philip who?
**Philip my glass please,
it's empty!**

Knock, knock ...
Who's there?
Butcher ...
Butcher who?
**Butcher money where your
mouth is!**

FUNNIEST JOKES
OF ALL!

Knock, knock ...
Who's there?
Galway ...
Galway who?
Galway, your annoying me!

Knock, knock ...
Who's there?
Alex ...
Alex who?
Alex the questions
round here!

Knock, knock ...
Who's there?
Athena ...
Athena who?
**Athena alien land
outside your house!**

Knock, knock ...
Who's there?
Zany ...
Zany who?
Zany body home?

Knock, knock ...
Who's there?
Button ...
Button who?
Button in is not polite!

43

Knock, knock ...
Who's there?
Fozzie ...
Fozzie who?
**Fozzie hundredth
time let me in!**

Knock, knock!

Knock, knock ...
Who's there?
Icon ...
Icon who?
**Icon tell you a
different knock,
knock joke if you like!**

Knock, knock ...
Who's there?
Doughnut ...
Doughnut who?
Doughnut ask, it's a secret!

Knock, knock ...
Who's there?
Urchin ...
Urchin who?
Urchin has food on it!

Knock, knock ...
Who's there?
Mickey ...
Mickey who?
**Mickey fell down the drain—
do you have a spare?**

Knock, knock ...
Who's there?
Woody ...
Woody who?
**Woody open the door
if I ask nicely?**

Knock, knock ...
Who's there?
Karl ...
Karl who?
**I'll Karl by another day
when you're feeling more friendly!**

Knock, knock ...
Who's there?
Jethro ...
Jethro who?
**Jethro the
key out of the
window and I'll
let myself in!**

Knock, knock ...
Who's there?
May ...
May who?
**Maybe its your best friend
at the door!**

**Knock,
knock!**

Knock, knock ...
Who's there?
Isadore ...
Isadore who?
**Isadore locked,
I can't get in!**

Knock, knock ...
Who's there?
Wanda ...
Wanda who?
**Wanda know how much longer you're
going to keep me waiting!**

Knock, knock ...
Who's there?
Juno ...
Juno who?
Juno what the time is, please?

Knock, knock ...
Who's there?
Cecile ...
Cecile who?
Cecile this envelope!

Knock, knock ...
Who's there?
Ivana ...
Ivana who?
Ivana be rich!

Knock, knock ...
Who's there?
Icing ...
Icing who?
Icing carols then you give me money!

Knock, knock ...
Who's there?
Jupiter ...
Jupiter who?
**Jupiter spaceship
on my lawn?**

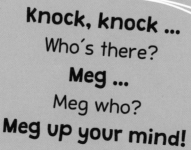

Knock, knock ...
Who's there?
Meg ...
Meg who?
Meg up your mind!

Knock, knock ...
Who's there?
Chris ...
Chris who?
**Chris-p lettuce goes soggy
if you leave it out!**

Knock, knock ...
Who's there?
Julia ...
Julia who?
**Julia want to come for
a run with me?**

Knock, knock ...
Who's there?
Otto ...
Otto who?
Ottold you who a minute ago!

Knock, knock ...
Who's there?
Izzy ...
Izzy who?
**Izzy come,
Izzy go!**

Knock, knock ...
Who's there?
Gandhi ...
Gandhi who?
Gandhi cane!

**Knock,
knock!**

Knock, knock ...
Who's there?
C-2 ...
C-2 who?
**C-2 it that you
don't forget
my name next
time!**

Knock, knock ...
Who's there?
Dino ...
Dino who?
Dino what you're having for supper—I can smell it from out here!

Knock, knock ...
Who's there?
Cash ...
Cash who?
No, thanks. I prefer walnuts.

Knock, knock ...
Who's there?
Hayden ...
Hayden who?
Hayden seek.

Knock, knock ...
Who's there?
Midas ...
Midas who?
Midas well open the door!

Knock, knock ...
Who's there?
Zeke ...
Zeke who?
Zeke and you shall find ...

Knock, knock ...
Who's there?
Alma ...
Alma who?
Alma-ny knock, knock jokes can you take?

53

Knock, knock ...
Who's there?
Albert ...
Albert who?
Albert you don't know who this is!

Knock, knock ...
Who's there?
Yul ...
Yul who?
Yuletide greetings to you!

Knock, knock ...
Who's there?
Jess ...
Jess who?
I give up, who?

Knock, knock ...
Who's there?
Noah ...
Noah who?
Noah don't know who you are either!

Knock, knock ...
Who's there?
Watson ...
Watson who?
Watson TV tonight?

Knock, knock ...
Who's there?
Wade ...
Wade who?
Wade a minute, I'll just check!

Knock, knock ...
Who's there?
Osborn ...
Osborn who?
Osborn today—it's my birthday!

Knock, knock ...
Who's there?
Mikey ...
Mikey who?
Mikey won't fit in this lock!

Knock, knock ...
Who's there?
Carmen ...
Carmen who?
Carmen get it!

Knock, knock ...
Who's there?
Freddie ...
Freddie who?
Freddie or not, here I come!

Knock, knock ...
Who's there?
Walter ...
Walter who?
**Walter strange
thing to ask!**

Knock, knock ...
Who's there?
Mort ...
Mort who?
**Mort to the point,
who are you?**

Knock, knock ...
Who's there?
Denise ...
Denise who?
Denise are cold—let me in!

Knock, knock ...
Who's there?
Jaffa ...
Jaffa who?
Jaffa keep me waiting?

Knock, knock ...
Who's there?
Glasgow ...
Glasgow who?
Glasgow to the movies!

Knock, knock ...
Who's there?
Handsome ...
Handsome who?
Handsome chips to me and I'll tell you more!

Knock, knock ...
Who's there?
Ears ...
Ears who?
Ears looking at you!

Knock, knock ...
Who's there?
Butch ...
Butch who?
Butch your arms around me!

Knock, knock ...
Who's there?
Lettuce ...
Lettuce who?
Lettuce in and you'll find out!

59

Knock, knock ...
Who's there?
Nana ...
Nana who?
Nana your business!

Knock, knock ...
Who's there?
Who ...
Who who?
Is there an owl in here?

Knock, knock ...
Who's there?
Jethro ...
Jethro who?
Jethro the boat and stop talking so much!

Knock, knock ...
Who's there?
Havelock ...
Havelock who?
Havelock put on your door!

Knock, knock ...
Who's there?
Posy ...
Posy who?
Posy open the door
and find out?

Knock, knock ...
Who's there?
Genoa ...
Genoa who?
Genoa any new jokes?
These are terrible!

SILLY JOKES!

Knock, knock ...
Who's there?
Jester ...
Jester who?
**Jester minute,
I'm trying to
find my keys!**

Knock, knock ...
Who's there?
Chester ...
Chester who?
**Chester man delivering
a parcel!**

Knock, knock …
Who's there?
Muffin …
Muffin who?
**Muffin the matter with me,
how about you?**

Knock, knock …
Who's there?
Felix …
Felix who?
**Felix my ice cream,
I'll lick his!**

Knock, knock …
Who's there?
Russell …
Russell who?
**Russell up a hot
drink, will you? It's
freezing out here!**

Knock, knock ...
Who's there?
Bolton ...
Bolton who?
Bolton the door is stuck, can you try to undo it?

Knock, knock ...
Who's there?
Carl ...
Carl who?
Carl get you there quicker than if you walk!

Knock, knock ...
Who's there?
Greta ...
Greta who?
You Greta on my nerves!

Knock, knock ...
Who's there?
Florinda ...
Florinda who?
**Florinda bathroom is wet,
so be careful!**

Knock, knock ...
Who's there?
Olivia ...
Olivia who?
Olivia, but I lost my key!

Knock, knock ...
Who's there?
Don Juan ...
Don Juan who?
**Don Juan to go to
school today!**

65

Knock, knock ...
Who's there?
Ferdie ...
Ferdie who?
Ferdie last time, open this door!

Knock, knock ...
Who's there?
Baby ...
Baby who?
**Baby I shouldn't hab come round
wiv dis cold!**

Knock, knock ...
Who's there?
Emma ...
Emma who?
**Emma going
to have to let
myself in?**

Knock, knock ...
Who's there?
Will ...
Will who?
Will wait out here until you let me in!

Knock, knock ...
Who's there?
Aida ...
Aida who?
**Aida lot of cake and
now I've got tummy ache!**

Knock, knock ...
Who's there?
Jilly ...
Jilly who?
Jilly out here—let me in!

68

Knock, knock ...
Who's there?
Brad ...
Brad who?
**Brad news I'm afraid—
your doorbell's broken!**

Knock, knock ...
Who's there?
Armageddon ...
Armageddon who?
**Armageddon getting
out of here!**

Knock, knock ...
Who's there?
Joan ...
Joan who?
**Joan you
remember me?**

**Knock,
knock!**

Knock, knock ...
Who's there?
Zubin ...
Zubin who?
Zubin eating garlic again?

Knock, knock ...
Who's there?
Despair ...
Despair who?
Despair is flat, do you have a pump I could borrow?

Knock, knock ...
Who's there?
May ...
May who?
May I come in?

70

Knock, knock ...
Who's there?
Alex ...
Alex who?
**Alex to surf.
What's your hobby?**

Knock, knock ...
Who's there?
Fred ...
Fred who?
**Fred you'll have
to let me in!**

Knock, knock ...
Who's there?
Adair ...
Adair who?
**Adair once, but
I'm bald now!**

71

Knock, knock ...
Who's there?
Posh ...
Posh who?
Posh the door open and you'll see!

Knock, knock ...
Who's there?
Leyland ...
Leyland who?
Leyland of the free and the home of the brave!

Knock, knock ...
Who's there?
Pecan ...
Pecan who?
Pecan someone your own size!

Knock, knock ...
Who's there?
Madrid ...
Madrid who?
Madrid you wash my jeans?

Knock, knock ...
Who's there?
Les ...
Les who?
**Les go for
a swim!**

Knock, knock ...
Who's there?
Esther ...
Esther who?
Esther anything I can do for you?

73

Knock, knock ...
Who's there?
Adolf ...
Adolf who?
**Adolf ball hit me in
de mouf!**

Knock, knock ...
Who's there?
Figs ...
Figs who?
**Figs the doorbell—my hand hurts
from all the knocking!**

Knock, knock ...
Who's there?
Waddle ...
Waddle who?
Waddle you give me if I go away?

Knock, knock ...
Who's there?
Bart ...
Bart who?
**Bart time you opened
this door!**

Knock, knock ...
Who's there?
Lena ...
Lena who?
**Lena little closer
and I'll tell you!**

Knock, knock ...
Who's there?
Ya ...
Ya who?
**What are you getting
so excited about?**

75

Knock, knock ...
Who's there?
Ears ...
Ears who?
Ears some more knock, knock jokes for you!

Knock, knock ...
Who's there?
Homer ...
Homer who?
Homer goodness—I can't remember myself!

Knock, knock ...
Who's there?
Borg ...
Borg who?
Borg out of my mind!

Knock, knock ...
Who's there?
Orange ...
Orange who?
Orange you glad
to see me?

Knock, knock ...
Who's there?
Europe ...
Europe who?
Europe to no
good!

Knock, knock ...
Who's there?
Mike ...
Mike who?
Mike car has a flat—can I come
in and use the phone?

Knock, knock ...
Who's there?
Chester ...
Chester who?
Chester minute—I'm in the wrong street!

Knock, knock ...
Who's there?
Miniature ...
Miniature who?
**Miniature open the door,
I'll tell you!**

Knock, knock ...
Who's there?
Lenny ...
Lenny who?
**Lenny in,
I'm hungry!**

Knock, knock ...
Who's there?
Ear ...
Ear who?
Ear you are! I've been looking for you!

Knock, knock ...
Who's there?
Al ...
Al who?
Al give you a kiss if you open this door!

Knock, knock!

Knock, knock ...
Who's there?
Alva ...
Alva who?
Alva heart and let me in!

EVEN SILLIER JOKES!

Knock, knock ...
Who´s there?
Superman ...
Superman who?
You know I can't reveal my secret identity!

Knock, knock ...
Who´s there?
Leaf ...
Leaf who?
Leaf me alone!

80

Knock, knock ...
Who's there?
Ice cream ...
Ice cream who?
**Ice cream every time
I see a ghost!**

Knock, knock ...
Who's there?
Essen ...
Essen who?
**Essen it fun listening
to these jokes?**

Knock, knock ...
Who's there?
Omar ...
Omar who?
**Omar goodness gracious,
I've got the wrong door!**

81

Knock, knock …
Who's there?
Lemon …
Lemon who?
Lemon me give you a kiss!

Knock, knock …
Who's there?
Emma …
Emma who?
**Emma bit cold
out here, can you
let me in?**

Knock, knock …
Who's there?
Alfie …
Alfie who?
Alfie terrible if you leave!

Knock, knock ...
Who's there?
Phyllis ...
Phyllis who?
Phyllis up a cup of water!

Knock, knock ...
Who's there?
Belle ...
Belle who?
**Belle don't work,
so I have to
knock!**

Knock, knock ...
Who's there?
Guess Simon ...
Guess Simon who?
**Guess Simon the
wrong doorstep!**

Knock, knock ...
Who's there?
Abbott ...
Abbott who?
**Abbott time you opened
this door!**

Knock, knock ...
Who's there?
Butter ...
Butter who?
Butter open quick, I need the bathroom!

Knock, knock ...
Who's there?
Sherlock ...
Sherlock who?
**Sherlock your door!
Someone could break in ...**

84

Knock, knock ...
Who's there?
Howell ...
Howell who?
Howell you have your pizza, plain or with pepperoni?

Knock, knock ...
Who's there?
Emmett ...
Emmett who?
Emmett your Service!

Knock, knock ...
Who's there?
Donna ...
Donna who?
Donna knock once more, then I'm going home!

Knock, knock ...
Who's there?
Giraffe ...
Giraffe who?
Giraffe to ask me that stupid question?

Knock, knock ...
Who's there?
Enid ...
Enid who?
Enid some more pocket money!

Knock, knock ...
Who's there?
Isabelle ...
Isabelle who?
Isabelle not working?

Knock, knock ...
Who's there?
Teresa ...
Teresa who?
Teresa jolly good fellow!

Knock, knock ...
Who's there?
Mae ...
Mae who?
Mae be I'll tell you, or Mae be I won't ...

Knock, knock ...
Who's there?
Candice ...
Candice who?
Candice joke get any worse?

Knock, knock ...
Who's there?
Hugo ...
Hugo who?
Hugo your way and I'll go mine!

Knock knock ...
Who's there?
Police.
Police who?
Police can you stand still, I'm trying to take your photo!

Knock, knock ...
Who's there?
Arnie ...
Arnie who?
Arnie ever going to let me in?

Knock, knock ...
Who's there?
Fitz ...
Fitz who?
Fitz not too much trouble, can you please open the door?

Knock, knock ...
Who's there?
You ...
You who?
Hello!

Knock, knock ...
Who's there?
Eyesore ...
Eyesore who?
Eyesore do like you!

Knock, knock ...
Who's there?
Elsie ...
Elsie who?
Elsie you around!

Knock, knock ...
Who's there?
Batman ...
Batman who?
You mean there's more than one?

Knock, knock ...
Who's there?
Belize ...
Belize who?
Belize in yourself!

Knock, knock ...
Who's there?
Teacher ...
Teacher who?
Teacher self for a few days, I'm off to France!

Knock, knock ...
Who's there?
Norma Lee ...
Norma Lee who?
**Norma Lee I have my key, but today
I left it at home.**

Knock, knock ...
Who's there?
Abbey ...
Abbey who?
**Abbey stung me
on the nose!**

Knock, knock ...
Who's there?
Ella Man ...
Ella Man who?
**Ella Man-tary my
dear Watson!**

Knock, knock ...
Who's there?
Ike ...
Ike who?
**Ike could have
danced all night ...**

Knock, knock ...
Who's there?
Bacon ...
Bacon who?
**Bacon a cake for
your birthday!**

Knock, knock ...
Who's there?
Sally ...
Sally who?
**Sally-brate the best moments
of your life!**

Knock, knock ...
Who's there?
Chaz ...
Chaz who?
**Chaz pass the key through the letterbox
and I'll open the door myself!**

Knock, knock ...
Who's there?
Perth ...
Perth who?
**Perth your lips
and whistle!**

**Knock,
knock!**

Knock, knock ...
Who's there?
Lionel ...
Lionel who?
**Lionel get you
nowhere, you'd
better tell the truth!**

Knock, knock ...
Who's there?
Ina ...
Ina who?
**Ina minute I'm going to knock
this door down!**

Knock, knock ...
Who's there?
Haifa ...
Haifa who?
**Haifa cake is better
than none!**

Knock, knock ...
Who's there?
Ben ...
Ben who?
**Ben knocking on this
door all morning!**

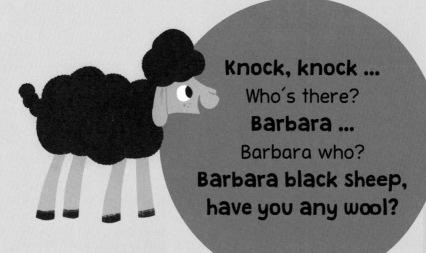

Knock, knock ...
Who's there?
Barbara ...
Barbara who?
**Barbara black sheep,
have you any wool?**

Knock, knock ...
Who's there?
I don't know ...
I don't know who?
**I told you I don't know. Why don't
you believe me?**

Knock, knock ...
Who's there?
Mary ...
Mary who?
**Mary Christmas,
ho, ho, ho!**

Knock, knock ...
Who's there?
Mike ...
Mike who?
**Mike up your mind!
Are you letting me
in or not?**

Knock, knock ...
Who's there?
Paul ...
Paul who?
**Paul the door from your
Side—it's a bit stiff!**

Knock, knock ...
Who's there?
Polly ...
Polly who?
**Polly door again,
it's still stuck!**

Knock, knock ...
Who's there?
Foster ...
Foster who?
Foster than the speed of light!

Knock, knock ...
Who's there?
Spock ...
Spock who?
**Spock the difference between me
and my twin brother!**

Knock, knock ...
Who's there?
Elias ...
Elias who?
Elias a terrible thing!

Knock, knock ...
Who's there?
Chuck ...
Chuck who?
Chuck the key under the door and I'll let myself in!

Knock, knock ...
Who's there?
Eamonn ...
Eamonn who?
Eamonn a good mood today, so can I come in?

Knock, knock ...
Who's there?
Ali ...
Ali, who?
Ali–ttle old man who can't reach the doorbell!

Knock, knock ...
Who's there?
Arnie ...
Arnie who?
**Arnie having
fun?**

Knock, knock ...
Who's there?
Eddie ...
Eddie who?
**Eddie body
home?**

Knock, knock ...
Who's there?
Scold ...
Scold who?
**Scold out—let's go play
in the snow!**

SILLIEST JOKES OF ALL!

Knock, knock ...
Who's there?
Khan ...
Khan who?
Khan you give me a lift to school? I'm late!

Knock, knock ...
Who's there?
Seymour ...
Seymour who?
Seymour of me by opening the door!

Knock, knock ...
Who's there?
Earl ...
Earl who?
Earl be glad to tell you when you open this door!

Knock, knock ...
Who's there?
Theodore ...
Theodore who?
Theodore wasn't open so I knocked!

Knock, knock ...
Who's there?
Dummy ...
Dummy who?
Dummy a good deed and go away!

Knock, knock ...
Who's there?
Sam ...
Sam who?
**Sam person who knocked
on the door last time!**

Knock, knock ...
Who's there?
Wendy ...
Wendy who?
**Wendy red, red robin comes bob,
bob bobbin' along, along ...**

Knock, knock ...
Who's there?
Tessa ...
Tessa who?
**Tessa long time for
you to open
the door!**

102

Knock, knock ...
Who's there?
Arthur ...
Arthur who?
Arthur any more purple jelly beans in the jar? They're the best!

Knock, knock ...
Who's there?
Hardy ...
Hardy who?
Hardy har, fooled you!

Knock, knock ...
Who's there?
Buddha ...
Buddha who?
Buddha this slice of bread for me, will you?

Knock, knock ...
Who's there?
Charlie ...
Charlie who?
Charlie you know the sound
of my voice by now!

Knock, knock ...
Who's there?
Zippy ...
Zippy who?
Zippy dee-doo-dah, zippy dee hey!

Knock, knock ...
Who's there?
Trixie ...
Trixie who?
Trixie couldn't do because
he was a bad magician!

Knock, knock ...
Who's there?
Usher ...
Usher who?
Usher wish you would let me in!

Knock, knock ...
Who's there?
Mabel ...
Mabel who?
Mabel is broken too ...

Knock, knock!

Knock, knock ...
Who's there?
Dwayne ...
Dwayne who?
Dwayne in Spain falls mainly on the plain!

Knock, knock ...
Who's there?
Farmer ...
Farmer who?
**Farmer distance
your house looks
much bigger!**

Knock, knock ...
Who's there?
Sid ...
Sid who?
**Sid down and
I'll explain!**

Knock, knock ...
Who's there?
Carl ...
Carl who?
**Carl my dad and ask him to
come and pick me up!**

Knock, knock ...
Who's there?
Moo ...
Moo, who?
**Make up your mind—
are you a cow
or an owl?**

Knock, knock ...
Who's there?
Element ...
Element who?
**Element to tell you that
she can't come round today.**

Knock, knock ...
Who's there?
Ahmed ...
Ahmed who?
**Ahmed a big mistake
coming here!**

Knock, knock ...
Who's there?
Courtney ...
Courtney who?
Courtney fish lately?

Knock, knock ...
Who's there?
Mandy ...
Mandy who?
Mandy lifeboats!

Knock, knock ...
Who's there?
Gary ...
Gary who?
Gary on smiling!

Knock, knock ...
Who's there?
Simon ...
Simon who?
Simon every occasion—you always make me wait!

Knock, knock ...
Who's there?
Major ...
Major who?
Major headache—are there any painkillers?

Knock, knock ...
Who's there?
Anna ...
Anna who?
Anna going to tell you, you'll have to keep guessing!

Knock, knock ...
Who's there?
Adelia ...
Adelia who?
Adelia the cards and we'll play snap!

Knock, knock ...
Who's there?
Misty ...
Misty who?
Misty doorbell again!

Knock, knock ...
Who's there?
Dunce ...
Dunce who?
Dunce-ay another word!

Knock, knock ...
Who's there?
Annetta ...
Annetta who?
**Annetta wisecrack
and you're out of here!**

Knock, knock ...
Who's there?
Ada ...
Ada who?
Ada hot dog for lunch!

Knock, knock ...
Who's there?
Juicy ...
Juicy who?
Juicy what I just saw?

Knock, knock ...
Who's there?
Phyllis ...
Phyllis who?
**Phyllis bag with
money,
I'm a robber!**

Knock, knock ...
Who's there?
Ray ...
Ray who?
**Ray-ning cats
and dogs.**

Knock, knock ...
Who's there?
Just Paul ...
Just Paul who?
**Just Pauling
your leg—it's
me, not Paul!**

Knock, knock ...
Who's there?
Douglas ...
Douglas who?
Douglas is broken in your front door!

Knock, knock ...
Who's there?
Yootha ...
Yootha who?
**Yootha person
with the
bike for sale?**

Knock, knock ...
Who's there?
Eye ...
Eye who?
Eye know who you are!

Knock, knock ...
Who's there?
Olive ...
Olive who?
Olive none of your lip!

Knock, knock ...
Who's there?
Violet ...
Violet who?
Violet the cat out of the bag?

Knock, knock ...
Who's there?
Dishes ...
Dishes who?
Dishes the life!

Knock, knock ...
Who's there?
Rather ...
Rather who?
Rather not come in, actually.

Knock, knock ...
Who's there?
Fanny ...
Fanny who?
**Fanny body calls,
I'm out.**

Knock, knock ...
Who's there?
Daryl ...
Daryl who?
Daryl never be another you ...

Knock, knock ...
Who's there?
Tex ...
Tex who?
Tex you ages to open the door!

Knock, knock ...
Who's there?
Alexia ...
Alexia who?
Alexia again to open this door!

Knock, knock ...
Who's there?
Paula ...
Paula who?
**Paula up the door
handle will you
and let me in!**

116

Knock, knock ...
Who's there?
Willy ...
Willy who?
**Willy let me use your
washing machine?
Mine's broken!**

Knock, knock ...
Who's there?
Hammond ...
Hammond who?
**Hammond eggs for
breakfast.**

Knock, knock ...
Who's there?
Egbert ...
Egbert who?
Egbert no bacon!

CRAZY JOKES!

Knock, knock ...
Who's there?
Carla ...
Carla who?
**Carla cab, we're
leaving!**

Knock, knock ...
Who's there?
Alpaca ...
Alpaca who?
**Alpaca the big case, you pack
the small one!**

Knock, knock ...
Who's there?
Aardvark ...
Aardvark who?
Aardvark a million
miles for one of
your smiles.

Knock,
knock!

Knock, knock ...
Who's there?
Pasture ...
Pasture who?
Pasture bedtime,
isn't it?

Knock, knock ...
Who's there?
Deanna ...
Deanna who?
Deanna-mals are restless, I think
they need feeding!

Knock, knock ...
Who's there?
Alma ...
Alma who?
**Alma not going to
tell you!**

Knock, knock ...
Who's there?
Waiter ...
Waiter who?
**Waiter minute while
I tie my shoelaces.**

Knock, knock ...
Who's there?
Yul ...
Yul who?
Yul see who when you open the door!

Knock, knock ...
Who's there?
Ozzie ...
Ozzie who?
**Ozzie you still have the same front door
as the last time I called!**

Knock, knock ...
Who's there?
Radio ...
Radio who?
**Radio not, here
I come!**

Knock, knock ...
Who's there?
Cook ...
Cook who?
**Who are you
calling cuckoo?**

Knock, knock ...
Who's there?
Mustapha ...
Mustapha who?
Mustapha good reason to keep me waiting so long!

Knock, knock ...
Who's there?
Lionel ...
Lionel who?
Lionel get angry if you don't feed him!

Knock, knock ...
Who's there?
Sherwood ...
Sherwood who?
Sherwood like to meet you!

Knock, knock ...
Who's there?
Passion ...
Passion who?
Passion through and thought I'd say hello!

Knock, knock ...
Who's there?
Althea ...
Althea who?
Althea later, alligator!

Knock, knock ...
Who's there?
Spell ...
Spell who?
W ... H ... O!

123

Knock, knock ...
Who's there?
Anita ...
Anita who?
Anita take the dog for a walk. Are you coming?

Knock, knock ...
Who's there?
Lisa ...
Lisa who?
Lisa you can do is let me in!

Knock, knock ...
Who's there?
Don Giovanni ...
Don Giovanni who?
Don Giovanni talk to me?

Knock, knock ...
Who's there?
Howard ...
Howard who?
**Howard you know
if you won't even open the door?**

Knock, knock ...
Who's there?
Courtney ...
Courtney who?
**Courtney door, can you open
it and let me free?**

Knock, knock ...
Who's there?
Hedda ...
Hedda who?
**Hedda nough of this—
I'm off!**

125

Knock, knock ...
Who's there?
Congo ...
Congo who?
Congo out, I'm grounded!

Knock, knock ...
Who's there?
Alvin ...
Alvin who?
**Alvin a great time,
how about you?**

Knock, knock ...
Who's there?
Scott ...
Scott who?
Scott nothing to do with you!

Knock, knock ...
Who's there?
Value ...
Value who?
Value be my Valentine?

Knock, knock ...
Who's there?
Donna ...
Donna who?
Donna expect you to remember me, it's been a while!

Knock, knock ...
Who's there?
Safari ...
Safari who?
Safari, so good ...

Knock, knock ...
Who's there?
Jerome ...
Jerome who?
Jerome at last!

Knock, knock ...
Who's there?
Cohen ...
Cohen who?
**Cohen to knock just once more,
then I'm going to give up!**

Knock, knock ...
Who's there?
Deduct ...
Deduct who?
Donald Deduct!

Knock, knock ...
Who's there?
Donatello ...
Donatello who?
Donatello'n me!

Knock, knock ...
Who's there?
Lass ...
Lass who?
How long have you been a cowboy?

Knock, knock ...
Who's there?
Disk ...
Disk who?
Disk is a recorded message. Please leave your message after the beep!

Knock, knock ...
Who's there?
Dan ...
Dan who?
Dan just stand there—let me in!

Knock, knock ...
Who's there?
Dishes ...
Dishes who?
Dishes a very bad joke!

Knock, knock ...
Who's there?
Ida ...
Ida who?
Ida bought a new doorbell when the last one broke!

Knock, knock ...
Who's there?
Bargain ...
Bargain who?
Bargain up the wrong tree!

Knock, knock ...
Who's there?
Hawaii ...
Hawaii who?
I'm fine, Hawaii you?

Knock, knock ...
Who's there?
Connor ...
Connor who?
Connor please open the door!

Knock, knock ...
Who's there?
Diesel ...
Diesel who?
Diesel teach me to go around knocking on doors!

Knock, knock ...
Who's there?
Amana ...
Amana who?
Amana bad mood!

Knock, knock ...
Who's there?
Colin ...
Colin who?
Colin in for a chat!

132

Knock, knock ...
Who's there?
Giselle ...
Giselle who?
**Giselle flowers, or have I got
the wrong shop?**

Knock, knock ...
Who's there?
Wendy ...
Wendy who?
**Wendy you want
me to walk your
dog again?**

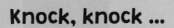

Knock, knock ...
Who's there?
Water ...
Water who?
Water you doing in my house?

Knock, knock ...
Who's there?
Imogen ...
Imogen who?
Imogen life without chocolate!

Knock, knock ...
Who's there?
Candy ...
Candy who?
Candy owner of this big red car come and move it off my drive!

Knock, knock ...
Who's there?
Chicken ...
Chicken who?
Chicken the oven, I can smell burning!

Knock, knock ...
Who's there?
Kay ...
Kay who?
Kay, L, M, N, O, P, Q, R, S, T, U, V, W, X, Y, Z!

Knock, knock ...
Who's there?
Lee King ...
Lee King who?
**Lee King bucket.
Can I borrow
yours?**

Knock, knock ...
Who's there?
Kent ...
Kent who?
**Kent you stop asking questions
and just open the door?**

Knock, knock ...
Who's there?
India ...
India who?
**India is some of my
stuff, and I've come
to collect it!**

**Knock,
knock!**

Knock, knock ...
Who's there?
Olive ...
Olive who?
Olive you!

Knock, knock ...
Who's there?
Alvin ...
Alvin who?
**Alvin your heart—just you
vait and see!**

Knock, knock ...
Who's there?
Dimension ...
Dimension who?
Dimension it!

Knock, knock ...
Who's there?
Linda ...
Linda who?
**Linda hand with my
suitcase please!**

Knock, knock ...
Who's there?
Andrew ...
Andrew who?
Andrew a picture for you!

EVEN CRAZIER
JOKES!

Knock, knock ...
Who's there?
Cereal ...
Cereal who?
Cereal pleasure to meet you!

Knock, knock ...
Who's there?
Veal chop ...
Veal chop who?
Veal chop around and see what bargains vee can pick up!

Knock, knock ...
Who's there?
Colin ...
Colin who?
Colin round to see you!

Knock, knock ...
Who's there?
Carla ...
Carla who?
Carla me please. We need to talk.

Knock, knock ...
Who's there?
Kline ...
Kline who?
**Kline of you to invite
me round!**

Knock, knock ...
Who's there?
Denver ...
Denver who?
**Denver the good
old days!**

Knock, knock ...
Who's there?
Peg ...
Peg who?
**Peg your pardon,
I've got the
wrong door!**

Knock, knock ...
Who's there?
Apple ...
Apple who?
**Apple your hair if
you don't let me in!**

Knock, knock ...
Who's there?
Heidi ...
Heidi who?
Heidi—Clare war on you!

Knock, knock ...
Who's there?
Ketchup ...
Ketchup who?
**Ketchup with me and
I will tell you.**

Knock, knock ...
Who's there?
Greta ...
Greta who?
**Greta friend like that again,
and you'll end up with none at all!**

Knock, knock ...
Who's there?
Kanga ...
Kanga who?
No! Kanga roo!

Knock, knock ...
Who's there?
Joanna ...
Joanna who?
Joanna have a guess?

Knock, knock ...
Who's there?
Woody ...
Woody who?
Woody lend me some money for an ice cream, please?

Knock, knock ...
Who's there?
Ivan ...
Ivan who?
Ivan idea you're going to keep me waiting out here a long time!

Knock, knock ...
Who's there?
McKee ...
McKee who?
McKee doesn't fit!

Knock, knock ...
Who's there?
Justin ...
Justin who?
Justin time to let me in!

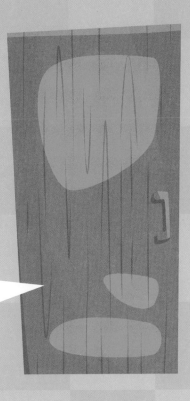

Knock, knock ...
Who's there?
Arch ...
Arch who?
You catching a cold?

Knock, knock ...
Who's there?
Paul ...
Paul who?
Paul the door open for goodness sake!

Knock, knock ...
Who's there?
Thermos ...
Thermos who?
Thermos be a better knock, knock joke than this!

Knock, knock ...
Who's there?
Whoo ooo oooo ooo ...
Whoo ooo oooo ooo who?
Great ghost impression!

Knock, knock ...
Who's there?
Bernadette ...
Bernadette who?
**Bernadette all my dinner so now
I'm starving!**

Knock, knock ...
Who's there?
Deena ...
Deena who?
Deena hear me knock?

145

Knock, knock …
Who's there?
Banana …
Banana who?
Knock, knock …
Who's there?
Banana …
Banana who?
Knock, knock …
Who's there?
Banana …
Banana who?
Knock, knock …
Who's there?
Orange …
Orange who?
**Orange you
glad I didn't say
banana?**

Knock, knock ...
Who's there?
Atlas ...
Atlas?
Atlas it's the weekend!

Knock, knock ...
Who's there?
Fletch ...
Fletch who?
**Fletch the fire brigade,
there's smoke coming
from your window!**

Knock, knock ...
Who's there?
Mouse ...
Mouse who?
**Mouse has burned down so
I'm coming to stay with you!**

Knock, knock ...
Who's there?
Amos ...
Amos who?
**Amos–quito is
chasing me—
please let me in!**

Knock, knock ...
Who's there?
Andy ...
Andy who?
Andy mosquito is chasing me again!

Knock, knock ...
Who's there?
Avenue ...
Avenue who?
**Avenue remembered you invited
me for lunch?**

148

Knock, knock ...
Who's there?
Honeybee ...
Honeybee who?
Honeybee a dear and open the door!

Knock, knock ...
Who's there?
Alex ...
Alex who?
Alex-plain when you open the door!

Knock, knock ...
Who's there?
Zeb ...
Zeb who?
Zeb better be a good reason for keeping me waiting out here!

Knock, knock ...
Who´s there?
I love ...
I love who?
I don't know, you tell me!

Knock, knock ...
Who´s there?
Darren ...
Darren who?
**Darren young man
on top of that
flying machine!**

Knock, knock ...
Who´s there?
Nadia ...
Nadia who?
**Nadia head if you understand
what I'm saying.**

Knock, knock ...
Who's there?
Sacha ...
Sacha who?
Sacha fuss, just because
I knocked on your door!

Knock, knock ...
Who's there?
Paula ...
Paula who?
Paula door open
and you'll see!

Knock, knock ...
Who's there?
Sid ...
Sid who?
Sid you'd be
ready by three—
you're late!

Knock, knock ...
Who's there?
Boliva ...
Boliva who?
Boliva me, I know what I'm talking about!

Knock, knock ...
Who's there?
Olly ...
Olly who?
Olly need is love!

Knock, knock ...
Who's there?
A little girl ...
A little girl who?
A little girl who can't reach the doorbell!

Knock, knock ...
Who's there?
Josie ...
Josie who?
Josie anyone else out here?

Knock, knock ...
Who's there?
Paul ...
Paul who?
Paul up a chair and I'll tell you!

Knock, knock ...
Who's there?
Axl ...
Axl who?
Axl me nicely and I might just tell you!

Knock, knock ...
Who's there?
Costas ...
Costas who?
**Costas a fortune
to get here.**

Knock, knock ...
Who's there?
Alma ...
Alma who?
**Alma time seems
to be spent on
this doorstep!**

Knock, knock ...
Who's there?
Doris ...
Doris, who?
**Doris locked, that's why I
had to knock!**

Knock, knock ...
Who's there?
Aunt Lou ...
Aunt Lou who?
Aunt Lou do you think
you are?

Knock, knock ...
Who's there?
Gorilla ...
Gorilla who?
Gorilla cheese
sandwich for me and
I'll be right over.

Knock, knock ...
Who's there?
Aaron ...
Aaron who?
Aaron on the side of caution!

CRAZIEST JOKES

OF ALL!

Knock, knock ...
Who's there?
U-8 ...
U-8 who?
U-8 my lunch!

Knock, knock ...
Who's there?
Avenue ...
Avenue who?
Avenue guessed yet?

Knock, knock ...
Who's there?
Bertha ...
Bertha who?
Bertha-day greetings!

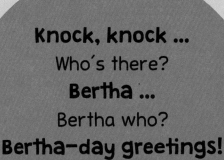

Knock, knock ...
Who's there?
Rabbit ...
Rabbit who?
Rabbit up carefully, it's a present!

Knock, knock ...
Who's there?
Annie ...
Annie who?
Annie one you like!

Knock, knock ...
Who's there?
Dale ...
Dale who?
Dale come if you ask dem!

Knock, knock ...
Who's there?
Formosa ...
Formosa who?
Formosa the summer I was away camping.

Knock, knock ...
Who's there?
Ginger ...
Ginger who?
Ginger hear the doorbell?

Knock, knock ...
Who's there?
Police ...
Police who?
Police let me in, it's cold out here.

Knock, knock ...
Who's there?
Cozy ...
Cozy who?
Cozy who's knocking!

Knock, knock ...
Who's there?
Josie ...
Josie who?
Josie any reason to keep me waiting out here?

Knock, knock ...
Who's there?
Cynthia ...
Cynthia who?
Cynthia you been away I missed you!

Knock, knock ...
Who's there?
Wendy ...
Wendy who?
Wendy wind blows de cradle will rock.

Knock, knock ...
Who's there?
Donald ...
Donald who?
Donald come baby, cradle and all ...

Knock, knock ...
Who's there?
Annie ...
Annie who?
Annie thing you can do, I can do better.

Knock, knock ...
Who's there?
Dexter ...
Dexter who?
Dexter halls with boughs of holly.

Knock, knock ...
Who's there?
Berlin ...
Berlin who?
**Berlin the water to cook
my eggs!**

Knock, knock ...
Who's there?
Ben ...
Ben who?
Ben wondering what you've been up to!

Knock, knock ...
Who's there?
Parton ...
Parton who?
Parton my French!

Knock, knock ...
Who's there?
Boo ...
Boo who?
**Don't cry, it's
only a joke!**

Knock, knock ...
Who's there?
Beets ...
Beets who?
Beets me!

Knock, knock ...
Who's there?
Jacklyn ...
Jacklyn who?
Jacklyn Hyde!

Knock, knock ...
Who's there?
Albee ...
Albee!
**Albee frozen if you leave me out
here much longer!**

Knock, knock ...
Who's there?
Queen ...
Queen who?
Queen as a whistle!

Knock, knock ...
Who's there?
Major ...
Major who?
**Major mind up whether you're going to
open the door yet?**

Knock, knock ...
Who's there?
Oman ...
Oman who?
**Oman, you are
cute!**

Knock, knock ...
Who's there?
Nobel ...
Nobel who?
Nobel, that's why I knocked!

Knock, knock ...
Who's there?
Ike ...
Ike who?
**Ike-an't stop
laughing!**

Knock, knock ...
Who's there?
Theodore ...
Theodore who?
Theodore is stuck and it won't open!

Knock, knock ...
Who's there?
Colleen ...
Colleen who?
**Colleen up this mess before I tell
your parents!**

Knock, knock ...
Who's there?
Dozen ...
Dozen who?
**Dozen anyone ever
answer the door!**

166

Knock, knock ...
Who's there?
Candy ...
Candy who?
Candy cow really jump over de moon?

Knock, knock ...
Who's there?
Cargo ...
Cargo who?
Cargo beep beep!

Knock, knock ...
Who's there?
Allied ...
Allied who?
Allied, I don't really want to come in!

Knock, knock ...
Who's there?
Amy ...
Amy who?
Amy fraid I've forgotten!

Knock, knock ...
Who's there?
Tennis ...
Tennis who?
Tennis five plus five!

Knock, knock ...
Who's there?
Alda ...
Alda who?
Alda time you knew I was waiting here!

Knock, knock ...
Who's there?
Celeste ...
Celeste who?
**Celeste time I'm going to
ask—please can you let me in?**

Knock, knock ...
Who's there?
Japan ...
Japan who?
Japan is too hot! Ouch!

Knock, knock ...
Who's there?
Alaska ...
Alaska who?
**Alaska the questions,
not you!**

Knock, knock ...
Who's there?
Delores ...
Delores who?
**Delores is on the side of
the good guys!**

Knock, knock ...
Who's there?
Lenny ...
Lenny who?
**Lenny in,
I'm hungry!**

Knock, knock ...
Who's there?
Alfred ...
Alfred who?
Alfred of the dark!

Knock, knock ...
Who's there?
Goose ...
Goose who?
Goose see a doctor, you don't look well!

Knock, knock ...
Who's there?
Colin ...
Colin who?
**Colin the doctor,
I feel ill!**

Knock, knock ...
Who's there?
Doctor ...
Doctor who?
**No, Doctor Smith.
I'm here to see the
patient ...**

Knock, knock ...
Who's there?
Frank ...
Frank who?
Frankenstein.
Arrrrgh!

Knock, knock ...
Who's there?
Jim ...
Jim who?
Jim mind if
I stay here
tonight?

Knock, knock ...
Who's there?
Cows go ...
Cows go who?
No, cows go moo!

Knock, knock ...
Who's there?
Chuck ...
Chuck who?
Chuck and see if the door is locked!

Knock, knock ...
Who's there?
Yachts ...
Yachts who?
Yachts up, doc?

Knock, knock ...
Who's there?
Alfred ...
Alfred who?
Alfred the needle and you sew!

Knock, knock ...
Who's there?
Alien ...
Alien who?
**Just how many
aliens do you know?**

Knock, knock ...
Who's there?
Lauren ...
Lauren who?
Lauren order!

Knock, knock ...
Who's there?
Howard ...
Howard who?
**Howard you like to be
outside for a change!**

Knock, knock ...
Who's there?
Eva ...
Eva who?
**Eva you're deaf or your doorbell
isn't working!**

Knock, knock ...
Who's there?
Accordion ...
Accordion who?
**Accordion to the weather forecast,
it's going to rain tomorrow!**

Knock, knock ...
Who's there?
Max ...
Max who?
Max no difference to me!

Knock, knock ...
Who's there?
Snow ...
Snow who?
Snow use—
I can't remember!

Knock, knock ...
Who's there?
Police ...
Police who?
Police stop telling these awful
knock, knock jokes!

Knock, knock ...
Who's there?
Gladys ...
Gladys who?
Gladys my last joke!